HAND

Tropical
Seashells

HANDY POCKET GUIDE TO
Tropical
Seashells

Text and photography by
Pauline Fiene-Severns
Mike Severns
Ruth Dyerly

PERIPLUS

Published by Periplus Editions (HK) Ltd.

Copyright © 2004 Periplus Editions (HK) Ltd.
ALL RIGHTS RESERVED
Printed in Singapore.
ISBN 0-7946-0193-6

Distributors

Indonesia
PT Java Books,
Jalan Kelapa Gading Kirana,
Blok A14/17, Jakarta 14240
Tel: 62 (021) 451 5352 Fax: 62 (021) 453 4987
Email: cs@javabooks.co.id

Japan
Tuttle Publishing
Yaekari Building 3F
5-4-12 Osaki, Shinagawa-ku
Tokyo 141-0032
Tel: (03) 5437 0171 Fax: (03) 5437 0755
Email: tuttle-sales@gol.com

North America, Latin America & Europe
Tuttle Publishing
364 Innovation Drive
North Clarendon, VT 05759-9436
Tel: (802) 773 8930 Fax: (802) 773 6993
Email: info@tuttlepublishing.com
www.tuttlepublishing.com

Asia Pacific
Berkeley Books Pte Ltd
130 Joo Seng Road, #06-01/03
Singapore 368357
Tel: (65) 6280 1330 Fax: (65) 6280 6290
Email: inquiries@periplus.com.sg

05 07 09 08 06 04
1 3 5 6 4 2

Introduction

Mollusks are found in a multitude of habitats, from the world's abyssal ocean plains to high in trees from which they never descend. They are sought for food by many animals including man, who considers some mollusks, such as calamari (squid) and oysters, a delicacy. This early cuisine was probably what brought shells to human camps, eventually to be used to create religious artifacts and for ornamentation such as exquisite cameos. Tools were also fashioned from sea shells, including drills made from the aptly-named auger shells, and adzes, fish-hooks and fish lures from various clams. Horns were made to call the people together or to scatter them to hide from an enemy.

Over 60,000 species of mollusks live in the Earth's seas, lakes, rivers and on land. A very diverse group, with equally diverse behaviors, the phylum Mollusca includes the fantastic chameleon-like octopus which mimics other animals and its surroundings; the free-swimming giant squid which lives in the dim twilight zone in deep ocean and is pursued by the equally giant sperm whale; bottom-burrowing clams, snails, slugs and the multi-hued nudibranchs, whose chemical defenses are now being studied for their medicinal properties.

Some mollusks defend themselves against foraging or curious humans by firing a venomous barb which is normally used to stun their fish prey. The toxin from a gland behind the barb of a fish-eating cone shell is injected at the same time the barb is pushed into its target and can occasionally be strong enough to kill a human. Mollusks can be grazers (such as the strombs and highly polished cowries), scavengers milling about looking for dead animals or ferocious predators. It is not hard to imagine how mollusks could have evolved so many specializations, since they have been around for over 500 million years.

The shells of most mollusk species are well known, but there is surprisingly little data on the behavior of some of these species. Behavioral observations may be far more valuable than collecting the shell when attempting to understand how these animals live. When shell collecting, the shell is taken and the animal thrown away. With the rising tide of human population, it is time to abandon the old idea of shell collecting for a more passive method of appreciating seashells by observation. If you must handle the shell, gently place it back where you found it to be sure it has a chance to survive.

Southeast Asia has an abundance of marine shells with the largest number of species in the world. Along the shores of seemingly countless islands and the coast of the Asian mainland it is not unusual to see spectacular and rare shells simply lying on the beaches. This book has been created to give beach-goers, snorkelers and divers a brief introduction to the sometimes fascinating shells they may find and a quick reference to those families of shells most often encountered. The entries are arranged in conventional taxonomic order.

Limpets

Family Acmaeidae/Fissurellidae

Above:
Patelloida saccharina,
Pacific sugar limpet,
27 mm

Below left:
Scutus unguis,
Hoof shield limpet,
24 mm

Below center:
*Diodora
quadriradiatus*, Four-
rayed keyhole limpet,
17 mm

Below right:
Patelloida saccharina,
Pacific sugar limpet,
27 mm

True limpets can be found along exposed rocky shore-lines, often above the low tide mark, exposed to air for hours at a time. The conical shell is held against the rock, conserving moisture, but is extended away from the rock when a wave crashes, to allow water to pass over the gills.

At high tide, when moisture loss is least likely, they move around grazing on algae. As the tide falls some species regularly return to a homesite of attachment where they have ground a circular place for themselves in the rock, which fits their shell. Years ago, a few mischievous scientists discovered that by changing the shape or surface features of a particular limpet's homesite, they could limit the ability of that limpet to identify it.

The related keyhole limpets must live at greater depths due to the hole in the top of the shell which would allow too much moisture loss if left exposed. Water exits through this hole after it has entered under the shell's lip and passed over the gills.

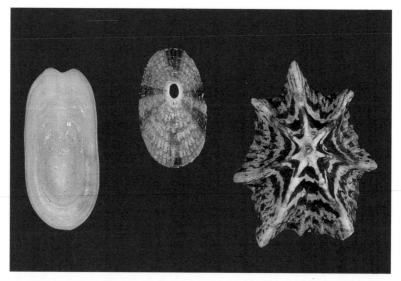

Abalones

Family Haliotidae

Most tropical abalones are small and thin-shelled, unlike the thick-shelled temperate abalones which are regularly harvested for food and for their opalescent shell interior. Abalones are usually found in shallow water beneath rocks on the shoreline and on reef flats from which they emerge at night to graze on algae.

They can crawl amazingly quickly. Close examination of the low, flat shell will reveal the characteristic spiral of a snail, with the aperture greatly expanded to accommodate the large, muscular, adhesive foot. Hundreds of tentacles protrude from the edge of the shell, presumably as sensory organs. During respiration, water is drawn in over the foot, passing beneath the lip of the shell over the gills, and is finally exhaled through a series of holes on the top of the shell.

Like the limpets, abalones are an early group in the evolution of mollusks, possessing a primitive type of gill structure and method of water circulation.

Above:
Haliotis varia,
Variable abalone,
21 mm

Below left:
Haliotis asinina,
Donkey's ear
abalone,
45 mm

Below right:
Haliotis ovina,
Oval abalone,
32 mm

Top Shells

Family Trochidae

Above:
Trochus niloticus,
Commercial top,
73 mm

Below left:
Tectus triserialis,
Tiered top
40 mm

Below center:
Trochus conus,
Cone top,
62 mm

Below right:
Trochus maculatus,
Maculated top,
35 mm

Top shells comprise a very large, diverse group of shells found from the shallow water of tide pools down to great depths. They generally have a shell that is thick and strong and, like the limpets, have evolved a high-spired, straight-sided shape that helps them hold on in surgy water. Most graze on seaweed and can be seen crawling about on the reef in shallow water at night.

When found by divers, most are heavily encrusted with calcareous (shell-like) deposits that hide the sculpture and color beneath. We recently encountered a top shell with the somewhat unusual habit of parasitizing black coral. Individuals appeared to be living on the black coral and stripping away the coral tissue.

Those species possessing an iridescent interior, especially the large *Trochus niloticus*, are harvested for commercial uses, including the manufacture of curios and pearl buttons that were very popular 100 years ago. These can still be found on some clothing as the fashion demands.

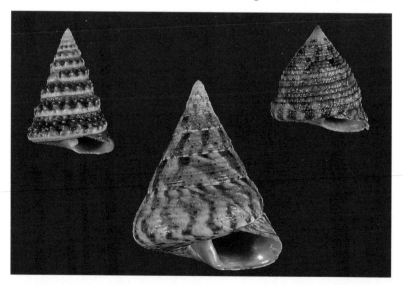

Turban Shells

Family Turbinidae

Turban shells are a large family with solid, globose shells that live in calm, shallow waters. They can be distinguished from the top shells by the operculum which is heavy and calcareous as opposed to thin and horny as in the top shells. Their rounded sides also distinguish them from the straight-sided top shells.

Many seashells have a "trap door" called an operculum, which protects the soft animal when it withdraws into its shell. In the turbans this operculum is heavily calcified and is sometimes called a "cat's eye." Unique and beautiful in its own right, this operculum alone can weigh as much as half a kilogram in the giant *Turbo marmoratus*.

Turban shells feed on microscopic algae by rasping them from hard surfaces, leaving a trail of clean substrate behind them. Accordingly they are most common on rocky bottoms where algae are profuse. Because of their substantial shell, empty turbans are likely to be found washed up, unbroken, on beaches.

Above:
Operculum
("cat's eye") from
Turbo chrysostomus,
Gold-mouth turban,
20 mm

Below left:
Turbo bruneus,
Brown Pacific turban,
50 mm

Below center:
Turbo petholatus,
Tapestry turban,
52 mm

Below right:
Turbo chrysostomus,
Gold-mouth turban,
53 mm

Nerites

Family Neritidae

Nerites are mainly intertidal species, living along the shoreline attached to rocks, mangrove roots or man-made structures from the splash zone on down into intertidal waters. Their distinguishing characteristic—a semicircular aperture, straight across one end—can be seen when viewed from beneath. This unusual aperture shape led to their common name of "slipper shells." The aperture is also characterized by strong tooth-like structures that are often splashed with color. Slipper shells are flattened, oval and thick-shelled, characteristics that allow them to survive the rugged conditions of the splash zone while remaining near their food source, the algae that thrive where sunlight and water exchange are greatest.

Some species are eaten by people after being heated and plucked from the shell with a sharp stick. Others are eaten raw as an intertidal hors d'oeuvre, but first one must get past a very tight-fitting calcareous operculum which protects the animal when it is withdrawn.

Periwinkles

Family Littorinidae

Periwinkles are the most common shells of the high shoreline where they graze on fine algae. Although capable of living above the high tide mark for long periods of time, they are tied to the ocean by the need to keep their gills moist and by their mode of reproduction. After mating, females either bear live young, lay a gelatinous egg mass, or shed fertilized eggs into the ocean where development takes place.

Above:
Littorina scabra,
Rough periwinkle,
19 mm

Below:
Littorina pintado,
Dotted periwinkle,
17 mm

Because they live exposed, they are rather small and drab so as not to attract the attention of predators. Some species can be found living on the leaves of mangrove trees, surprisingly high out of the water. The name "periwinkle" comes from the Elizabethan words "penny winkle," meaning small whelks that used to cost a penny per handful. Since they live in large colonies, often out of the water, they have been an abundant, easily collected food for many peoples for generations. They have also been commonly used for adornment.

Horn Shells

Family Cerithiidae

Above:
Clypeomorus coralium,
Coral horn shell,
25 mm

Below left:
Cerithium echinatum,
Spiny horn shell,
42 mm

Below center:
Pseudovertagus aluco,
Aluco horn shell,
57 mm

Below right:
Rhinoclavis sinensis,
Obelisk horn shell,
46 mm

Horn shells are a large group characterized by an up-turned canal in their shell that protects the siphon and allows them to live just beneath the surface of the sand. They are some of the most commonly-seen and abundant seashells in shallow water. At shallow depths the smaller species prefer to live in sand pockets and calm, protected bays, while the larger species are normally found in open sand beyond the reef.

These shallow-water dwellers can best be seen in the early morning before wind-driven waves and tides obliterate the trails left in the sand from the evening's foraging. The trails of deeper-water dwellers can be found throughout the day.

All are algae and detritus feeders and are common prey for predatory mollusks, especially moon shells which drill a hole through the shell and extract the animal. Hundreds of drilled horn shells, occupied by hermit crabs, can sometimes be seen on the reef flat at low tide.

True Conchs

Family Strombidae

Stromboids are named for the U-shaped (stromboid) notch at the front (bottom in the photo) end of the outer lip. One of the eyes is held upright, protruding through the notch in the shell, while the other is kept low, beneath the lip of the shell. The eyes are well developed and the animal responds quickly to movement and light changes. True conchs are herbivorous and are usually shallow-water dwellers. Because of their weight they are able to live on the reef flat without being tumbled as easily by water movement. Many of the larger common species are edible.

The true conchs have several unusual means of locomotion. One species, *Strombus maculatus*, has been known to leap farther than 1 m by digging its large operculum into the bottom and catapulting itself off the bottom. Another very unusual member of this family, *Terebellum terebellum*, is shaped like a bullet and can propel itself rapidly away from the bottom for up to 3 m, by flapping its fleshy foot.

Above:
Strombus aurisdianae,
Diana conch,
61 mm

Below left:
Strombus urceus,
Little bear conch,
54 mm

Below center:
Strombus lentiginosus,
Silver conch,
64 mm

Below right:
Strombus luhuanus,
Strawberry conch,
52 mm

Spider Conchs

Family Strombidae

Above:
Lambis crocata,
Orange spider conch,
105 mm

Below left:
Lambis millepeda,
Milleped spider
conch,
130 mm

Below center:
Lambis chiragra,
Chiragra spider
conch,
180 mm

Below right:
Lambis scorpius,
Scorpio conch,
140 mm

The unusual movement of the true conchs is eye-catching. Instead of gliding smoothly across the bottom as most snails do, they move by means of a strong, curved operculum (the trap door which protects the animal when it is withdrawn). The operculum is dug into the sand and the muscular foot hoists the shell up in a jerky, leaping motion up over the foot.

The spider conchs are characterized by long and thick, yet elegantly curved spinose projections along the lip of the shell. These are reef flat and shallow water dwellers which live out in the open, but algae and encrusting organisms growing on the outside of the shells manage to disguise them and make them difficult to see even though the shells are quite large. The flared edge of the shell protects the proboscis (feeding tube) which sweeps across the bottom in search of food. The sexes can often be distinguished by the form of the spines, with females possessing the longer spinose projections.

Carrier Shells

Family Xenophoridae

Carrier shells are a very old group which has been around since the Cretaceous period 135 million years ago. They have the amazing habit of cementing empty shells, coral or stones to their own shells with a type of nacreous glue secreted by the mantle as the shell forms. This practice may have developed as a protective measure, camouflaging the carrier shell from predators. Some species even attach branching sponges half a meter high!

Several adaptations indicate that carrier shells live on silty ocean floors—among these, a muscular foot which moves the animal around on the bottom with a jerky, leaping motion, and powerful currents produced in the mantle cavity to keep the cavity free of silt. Their silt habitat is further confirmed by the shell species that they have attached to their shells—these also inhabit silty areas. Carrier shells are mostly brought to light in trawls from very deep water and therefore information on their habits and behavior is limited.

Above and below: *Xenophora neozelanica*, Carrier shell, 68 mm

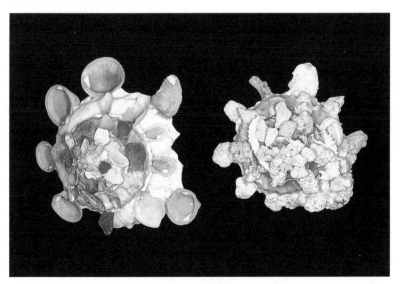

Large Cowries

Family Cypraeidae

Above:
Cypraea talpa,
Mole cowrie,
55 mm

Below left:
Cypraea tigris,
Tiger cowrie,
90 mm

Below center:
Cypraea mappa ,
Map cowrie,
84 mm

Below right:
Cypraea argus,
Eyed cowrie,
62 mm

Cowrie shells have long been prized by collectors for their high gloss, beautiful colors and intricate patterns. In India they were used as currency as early as A.D. 900 and the common name cowrie began as "kauri," the Hindu word for shells. Their use has been documented even earlier in China—in the 14th century B.C. *Cypraea moneta*, the "money cowrie," was used primarily, but other small, easily-gathered cowries were traded as well.

Cowries are characterized by their globose and glossy shells, narrow aperture and toothed lips. They live from the intertidal zone down to over 100 m and may remain in a small area during their relatively long life. Most species are active at night. After mating, the female lays her eggs in a protected depression or under a rock, and broods them by sitting for days with her foot spread over them. At first the eggs are white, but as they mature they turn dark gray. Some large cowries may live ten years or more and small ones two or three years.

Small Cowries

Family Cypraeidae

The beautiful luster of cowrie shells owes itself to the two lobes of the mantle which extend up on either side, covering and protecting the shell. When moving about, the mantle helps to camouflage the shell with its many projecting papillae. These papillae also function in respiration by adding surface area to the mantle, increasing oxygen exchange.

Most cowries feed on algae, sponges or dead animals such as fish, urchins or shrimp. Tangle nets are often used in the Philippines to collect those species that feed on dead animals. The narrow, toothy slit on the underside makes it difficult for predators to get at the animal, but they still fall prey to the occasional octopus which relishes the large tiger cowrie. In some oceanic cultures tiger cowrie shells are still used as bait to catch octopus. Deep-living fish sometimes swallow cowries whole and specimens taken from their stomachs may represent the only known examples of some rare species.

Above:
Cypraea asellus,
Horse cowrie,
18 mm

Below from left:
Cypraea cribraria,
Sieve cowrie,
28 mm

Cypraea moneta,
Money cowrie,
24 mm

Cypraea isabella,
Isabelle cowrie,
23 mm

Cypraea nucleus,
Nucleus cowrie,
24 mm

Egg Shells

Family Ovulidae

**Above
and below left**:
Ovula ovum,
Common egg shell,
90 mm

Below top right:
Calpurnus verrucosus,
Umbilical egg shell,
28 mm

Below bottom right:
Calpurnus lacteus,
Milk egg shell,
15 mm

The larger egg shells have the same basic shell characteristics as the smaller ovulids, but one, the common egg shell, has achieved a remarkable size (up to 100 mm in length). In contrast to its solid white shell, the animal is black with white speckling. The living egg shells can be found by looking on their food sources. They feed on large colonial soft corals and their presence is often given away by damaged coral tissue where the egg shell has eaten, or by the presence of its spherical eggs which are attached to its host coral. Since the corals on which the shells live are light in color, the black color of the animal is fairly easy to see.

They differ from the smaller ovulids in that they will travel across the bottom from one coral to another in search of food. The smaller ovulids generally remain on a very specific coral or gorgonian where they are perfectly camouflaged. Egg shells are generally found resting on the bottom in shallow water on or near their food source.

Ovulids

Family Ovulidae

Also known as allied cowries, the ovulids differ from cowries by their more extended ends, lack of a toothed aperture and lack of detailed color patterns. The shells of most ovulids are somewhat glossy because, like the cowries, the mantle covers the shell and keeps organisms from settling on it. Unlike the cowries, however, the mantle covers the shell even when it is inactive.

The ovulids are all carnivorous, feeding on hard corals, soft corals and gorgonians. Each species of ovulid has a specific host which it mimics in appearance so closely that when the animal is extended to cover the shell, it is extremely difficult to see.

Ovulids also lay their eggs on their host, either on the trunk of the coral or hanging like ornaments from the limbs of some branching gorgonians. This is often the only way that their presence is noticed. They range from intertidal to extremely deep depths and are found any place that soft corals are found.

Above:
Phenacovolva rosea,
Rosy ovulid,
50 mm

Clockwise from left:
Dentiovula dorsuosa,
Ridged ovulid,
17 mm

Pseudosimnia culmen,
Globose ovulid,
14 mm

Prosimnia semperi,
Semper ovulid,
16 mm

Crenavolva tigris,
Tiger ovulid,
11 mm

Moon Shells

Family Naticidae

Above:
Natica violacea,
Violet moon,
15 mm

Below left:
Polinices melanostomus,
Black-mouth moon,
26 mm

Below center:
Mamilla simiae,
Monkey moon,
15 mm

Below right:
Polinices tumidus,
Pear-shaped moon,
22 mm

Rarely seen, moon shells are sand-dwellers which lay a distinctively-shaped egg mass at night consisting of eggs, sand and mucus molded together into a flat, flexible collar. The moon shell then retreats into the sand, leaving the eggs exposed.

The animal is usually uniformly white, large and slimy and is often too large to fit entirely inside the shell. It lives in darkness beneath the sand, pulling itself along with a broad foot. Sand is kept out of the mantle cavity by the foot which covers the head region. Because the shells are always under sand or encased by the animal, the shells are almost always glossy and free from encrustation.

They prey on other sea shells, including horn shells, by boring a hole through the shell using a chemical secreted at the tip of the proboscis. This hole is the trademark of moon shell predation and if a dead shell is found on the reef with a conical hole in its side, then you can suspect its demise was precipitated by a moon shell.

Helmet Shells

Family Cassidae

Most members of this family are small sand-dwellers but a few members grow to impressive sizes and weights. The shells are heavily calcified and have teeth either just inside the lip or along the very outer edge. In the case of the horned helmet, *Cassis cornuta*, the males can be distinguished from the females by the height of the horns. Long-horned shells are males and short-horned shells are females. This is one of the few seashells large enough to have been used traditionally as a trumpet.

Helmets live mostly on open sand bottoms where they often spend their time buried in the sand when not hunting. Their prey consists primarily of sand-dwelling sea urchins and sand dollars, which they locate chemically. After the prey is located, they begin by removing the spines from an area on the urchin or sand dollar then bore a hole through which to extract the animal. A wake of empty urchin tests can often lead right to the responsible helmet shell.

Above:
Phalium decussatum,
Decussate bonnet,
57 mm

Below left:
Cypraecassis rufa,
Cameo helmet,
93 mm

Below right:
Cassis cornuta
Horned helmet,
94 mm

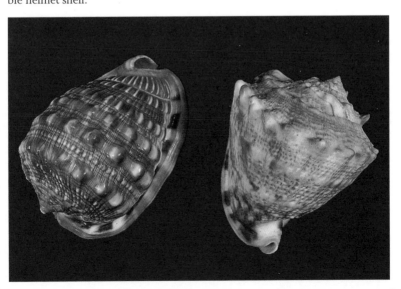

Tun shells

Family Tonnidae

Above:
Tonna perdix,
Partridge tun,
100 mm

Below left:
Tonna dolium,
Spotted tun,
118 mm

Below center:
Malea pomum,
Pacific grinning tun,
60 mm

Below right:
Tonna sulcosa,
Banded tun,
106 mm

Tun shells are characterized by their clean, thin, globular shells which usually have complex color patterns. In the case of *Tonna perdix* this has led to the choice of its scientific name. *Perdix* means quail-like and refers to the distinctive pattern on the shell. Most tun shells are large and it is hard to believe that shells of this size live under the sand, but they do! They move about much the same as the moon shells described earlier, and like the moon shells, some tun shell animals are so large that they cannot fit entirely into their shells.

This animal is a subtle hunter, coming out of the sand at night to feed on sleeping fish, echinoderms and crustaceans, by creeping up and pouncing on them with its large foot. Tun shells move along the top of the sand hunting for food and can quickly bury themselves in the sand when threatened. The only time one might encounter a living tun shell is at night, as there is no trace of them on the surface of the sand during the day.

Tritons

Family Cymatiidae

Some of the world's largest living seashells are included in this family which contains the triton's trumpet, *Charonia tritonis*, the second largest seashell in the Indo-West Pacific, sometimes reaching 500 mm! Although there are many species of triton, the triton's trumpet is by far the most well known. It is the shell most often used as a horn by peoples throughout the Pacific because of its size, beauty and the clear notes that can be produced.

Triton's trumpets are predators, feeding on a variety of mollusks, echinoderms and worms. Watching a triton's trumpet sense and track its prey is an education. It seems to come alive when it picks up the chemical signature of its prey, first extending from its shell, then following the chemical scent quickly until it reaches the prey and grabs it with its powerful foot. Then, like all tritons, it secretes a powerful, paralyzing acid from glands in its proboscis and slowly begins to digest its unlucky prey. They are long-lived and can be seen in one area for long periods of time.

Above:
Charonia tritonis,
Triton's trumpet,
200 mm

Below left:
Cymatium exile,
Exile triton,
56 mm

Below center:
Cymatium pyrum,
Pear triton,
85 mm

Below right:
Cymatium rubeculum,
Ruby triton,
40 mm

Fig Shells

Family Ficidae

These sand-dwelling shells get their name from their pear or fig shapes. Like many other shells that live under the protection of the sand, the shell is very light, thin, fragile to the touch and intricately patterned. The delicate lip is not thickened and the aperture runs the entire length of the shell. An elongated siphonal canal helps protect the siphon from predators while it is extended to "sniff" the water for chemicals given off by prey.

Because of their fragile shells, they are rarely found intact, whether while diving or looking on the beach. Fig shells are slender versions of the closely-related tun shells, both having a large animal and no protective operculum. Since they live under sand, their shells, like those of the tuns, are also free of foreign growth.

The animal has two large muscular lobes which it uses for locomotion while buried in the sand during the day, or out hunting on the sand surface at night. They feed primarily on sand-dwelling worms.

Toad Shells

Family Bursidae

The knobbed surface of these shells has resulted in the common family name "toad shells" probably because they resemble the bumps on a toad's back. The toad shells are characterized by a series of abandoned siphonal canals protruding from the spiraling folds of the shell. These were created and abandoned as the shell grew with only one in use at a time. The siphons all lie on the same plane, protruding to the right or the left of the shell indicating that it has growth spurts in which a half turn of new shell is laid down at a time.

    These growth periods are quiet times for the toad shell, when it will find a good hiding place and remain there until the new shell has formed and thickened. Like the tritons, toad shells possess an acid secretion with which they paralyze their prey of various worms. They can be found from shallow tide pools to extremely deep water and are most often heavily encrusted with coralline algae and other organisms.

Above:
Bursa bubo,
Giant toad shell,
240 mm

Below left:
Bursa lamarcki,
Lamarck's toad shell,
49 mm

Below center:
Bursa rubeta,
Ruddy toad shell,
87 mm

Below right:
Bursa cruentata,
Blood-stained toad shell,
36 mm

Wentletraps

Family Epitoniidae

Below:
Epitonium scalare,
Precious wentletrap,
47 mm

There is a legend that during the 19th century the precious wentletrap, *Epitonium scalare*, was so highly prized by collectors that paste imitations were made by Chinese craftsmen and sold as the real thing. Today those paste imitations would be worth far more than the real shell, since the shell turned out to be not-so-rare after its habitat was discovered. Unfortunately we could not find even one of the legendary paste wentletraps nor anyone who had ever seen one. Today, there are paste imitations being made in Taiwan, though they would never pass for the original shell as the legendary imitations reportedly did.

Wentletraps are generally foraging predators though some are permanent parasites on corals and anemones. They have a wide depth range from tide pools to very deep water. The name wentletrap comes from the Dutch word, "wenteltreppe," meaning spiral stairway because of the pronounced ribbing and open whorls of the shell.

Purple Sea Snails

Family Janthinidae

Instead of crawling on the bottom, these snails live their entire adult lives at the surface of the sea. A lightweight shell is buoyed by a float constructed of mucus-covered bubbles. To form the float, the snail extends its foot above the water, capturing a bit of air which it quickly encases in mucus. Many mucus-coated bubbles form the raft.

They feed on other organisms which float at the surface such as Portuguese-man-o-war and by-the-wind sailors. Since they cannot swim they are entirely dependent on the wind and current to bring them into contact with prey and mates. Fortunately, the bubble raft and the floats and sails of the prey are equally affected by these environmental forces and so prey is kept nearby.

The unusual lavender color of the shell and the animal helps it to blend with the color of the open ocean, perhaps camouflaging the sea snail from fish or birds. At the mercy of wind and waves, these shells are often washed up on beaches after storms at sea.

Below left:
Janthina janthina,
Common janthina,
27 mm

Below right:
Janthina globosa,
Globose janthina,
23 mm

Murex Shells

Family Muricidae

Above:
Chicoreus brunneus,
Burnt murex,
62 mm

Below left:
Murex tribulus,
Comb murex,
104 mm

Below center:
Chicoreus saulii,
Saul's murex,
90 mm

Below right:
Naquetia triquetra,
Triquetra murex,
55 mm

This very diverse family ranges from the delicate and spinose comb murexes to the heavy rock shells. The very long end protects the siphon which can poke into places looking for food. The shells of this group have the most complexly sculptured shapes of all the seashells.

The comb murexes inhabit sand, mud or rubble bottoms. Burnt murexes inhabit sand or rock substrate. All these spines may discourage predation by fish or other snail-drilling shells, but they also make movement across the bottom complicated. So the animal stretches out, holding the shell high above the bottom, and glides along. Murexes are carnivorous and feed on other seashells, corals, barnacles and echinoderms. They also secrete an acid which aids in boring through shell. The spines can even be used as a wedge to pry open clam shells.

In ancient times some species of murex were harvested by the Phoenicians and Egyptians to extract a purple dye used to color cloth.

Rock Shells

Family Muricidae

The rock shells live along rocky shorelines usually exposed to rough water, and thus lack the elaborate projections of other murexes which would only catch the water and make them more likely to be torn from the rock. The top and sides of their shells are often plain and heavily encrusted with coralline algae, making them difficult to distinguish from their background. However, when removed from the rocks, the underside of many species is colorful and lustrous. The foot is enlarged in those living on continuously wave-swept shores and small in those living in the calmer waters of tide pools.

The moon shells and rock shells, the two best-known groups of shell borers, bore a hole through their prey's shell to get at the animal inside. They feed mostly on shells that live on exposed shorelines such as periwinkles, nerites, limpets and barnacles. Deeper dwellers feed on worms and urchins. Their weighty shells are favored by hermit crabs because they provide good protection.

Above:
Drupa ricinus,
Prickly drupe,
25 mm

Clockwise from left:
Thais mancinella,
Mancinella rock shell,
50 mm

Drupa rubusidaeus,
Strawberry drupe,
38 mm

Nassa serta,
Wreath jopas,
50 mm

Thais tuberosa,
Tuberose rock shell,
47 mm

Coral Shells

Family Coralliophilidae

Above:
Coralliophila costularis,
Ribbed coral shell,
23 mm

Below left:
Coralliophila erosa,
South Seas coral shell,
25 mm

Below center:
Coralliophila pyriformis,
Pyriform coral shell,
36 mm

Below right:
Coralliophila neritoidea,
Violet coral shell,
20 mm

Coral shells, as their name suggests, live in close association with corals. Many species live permanently on coral, eating coral tissue and leaving tell-tale scars. Fortunately for these permanent coral dwellers, many individuals often live on the same coral colony, making potential mates accessible.

Some, like the *Latiaxis*, can be pure white except for their aperture which may have a touch of color within. If these shells lead a protected life the delicate, lacy sculpturing of the shell remains undamaged. Others like *Coralliophila violacea* that live a sedentary lifestyle attached to a coral host, can become heavily encrusted with calcium deposits. These deposits can completely obscure even the shape of the shell. However the side of the shell attached to the coral remains clean and the lip and aperture are often a deep, shiny purple. The females of this species keep the eggs under their shells until hatching, a habit considered unique to the family Coralliophilidae.

Whelks

Family Buccinidae

This is a large and diverse family with fusiform shells, a few of which exceed 50 mm. They range from tide pools to great depths and from tropical waters to the arctic. Though almost all seashells are dextral, or right-hand whorled, the whelks have several members of their family that have a left-handed, or sinistral, whorl. In some cultures a left-handed shell is said to bring good luck and so left-handed species are highly prized.

Whelks are active predators which feed on other mollusks and some crustaceans. They are also scavengers and are occasionally attracted to fishermen's traps and hauled up as a by-product of the day's catch.

Some live buried in the sand and others live exposed on the reef flat where their shells become encrusted with other living organisms, obscuring the sculpture and often the bright colors of the shells. Most have a thick, brittle operculum (horny plate) which protects the animal when it withdraws into its shell.

Above:
Pisania ignea,
Flame whelk,
36 mm

Below left:
Cantharus wagneri,
Wagner's goblet,
23 mm

Below center:
Cantharus undosus,
Waved goblet,
40 mm

Below right:
Phos textum,
Woven phos,
22 mm

Nassa Mud Snails

Family Nassariidae

Above:
Nassarius pullus,
Black nassa,
20 mm

Below left:
Nassarius glans,
Glans nassa,
50 mm

Below center:
Nassarius coronatus,
Crown nassa,
23 mm

Below right:
Nassarius papillosus,
Pimpled nassa,
46 mm

Characteristic of this group is their long siphon which they wave about as they move across the bottom in order to detect prey, which usually consists of decaying animals such as fish and crabs. They also hunt for living prey such as bivalves. Once these animals have located food, they are drawn like a magnet with surprising speed. They are so attuned to the scent that one decomposing prey item often attracts many mud snails.

As their name suggests, they are mostly shallow water mud- and sand-dwellers. The foot can be used to lash at predators in defense. This activity appears not so much designed to hurt the predator as to push the snail away. When they are knocked onto their sides, they will thrash around with their foot until they get a purchase in the sand and are able to right themselves.

At night they are quite active and the beauty of the remarkably colorful living animals can be seen as they crawl across the bottom.

Tulip & Spindle Shells

Family Fasciolariidae

The living animals of this group are unusually red-pigmented. Some can reach as much as 600 mm in length and live at great depths.

These are ferocious and active carnivores that emerge from beneath the sand during the late afternoon and early evening to hunt for crabs and other sand-dwelling animals. They move surprisingly quickly along the sand and may cover large areas during their search for food. Waves of fine muscular contractions in the foot propel the snails along. In the trough of the wave, the foot is lifted and returned to the bottom a little ahead of the previous position. Many waves of contractions produce a slow, but smooth fluid motion.

A thin, smooth layer of horny protein material coats the semi-glossy shell, which reduces friction when moving through sand and prevents the colonization of encrusting organisms on the outer surface. They lay beautiful, distinctive, vase-shaped egg cases.

Above:
Pleuroploca trapezium,
Trapezium horse
conch,
200 mm

Below left:
Latirus gibbulus,
Gibbose latirus,
80 mm

Below center:
*Pleuroploca
filamentosa*,
Filamentous horse
conch,
120 mm

Below right:
Latirus polygonus,
Polygon latirus,
74 mm

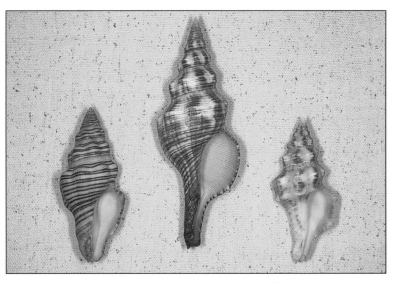

Dove Shells

Family Columbellidae

Above:
Aesopus spiculum,
Pointed dove shell,
14 mm

Below left:
Pyrene flava,
Yellow dove shell,
19 mm

Below center:
Pyrene punctata,
Telescoped dove shell,
22 mm

Below right:
Columbella scripta,
Script dove shell,
17 mm

Although small, most species of dove shells generally have polished, fusiform shells that are often quite colorful and unusually patterned. Many are so individually variable within the species that they have presented problems for taxonomists. Some confusion has resulted as several names were given to the same species.

Not only are dove shells varied in shape and color pattern, but they are also varied in their habits. Many are herbivorous, and can often be found on algae which they rasp with tiny, chitinous teeth, while others are carnivorous, feeding on anemones. Especially active at night, these shells can be seen most often foraging for food in the evening on sand and among rocks. During the day some species are found on sand while others can be found clinging to the undersides of rocks in tide pools and down to moderate depths. Dove shells lay hemispherical eggs on the hard surfaces beneath rocks, in cracks and other protected places.

Volutes

Family Volutidae

Considered the aristocrats of shells, volutes are among the most highly sought after and beautiful shells. Unlike many seashells, however, the large, living animals are just as beautiful, if not more so, than the shells, with outrageous colors and patterns and a long, protruding siphon which they follow with the same intensity as a dog will follow its nose.

The volute is a fast-moving carnivore that feeds on large crabs and even occasionally sleeping fish, killing its prey in much the same fashion as the harp shell, by enveloping and suffocating the prey with its foot. Usually found in deep water, a few species can be seen in snorkeling depths in the early evening and at night. Volutes are closely related to harp shells and, like the harp shells, they remain buried in the sand most of their lives, keeping the shell clean and relatively free of foreign growth. Because they attain such great size, they have been used by people for cupping water and are also known as "baler shells."

Above:
Cymbiola aulica,
Cathcart's volute,
75 mm

Below left:
Melo aethiopica,
Crowned baler,
200 mm

Below right:
Melo melo,
Indian volute,
120 mm

Olive Shells

Family Olividae

Above:
Oliva tessellata,
Tessellate olive,
22 mm

Below left:
Oliva reticulata,
Blood olive,
36 mm

Below center:
Oliva oliva,
Common olive,
27 mm

Below right:
Oliva annulata,
Amethyst olive,
35 mm

Super-glossy with a distinctive cylindrical shape, olive shells are easily recognized. The shell maintains such gloss in the same manner that cowries do. Two lobes of the mantle fold up over the shell, protecting the glazed surface. The narrow slit opening makes it difficult for a predator such as a crab to get at the animal.

Most are sand-dwellers occurring locally in large numbers and can be found by following their raised trails as they move just beneath the surface of the sand. They can even be found on the beach as the tide recedes, exposing their trails. The siphon, which is extended above the surface of the sand, allows the olive to sense food on the surface. The olive will then come to the surface, engulf the prey with its foot, smother it in slime and take it under the sand to eat where other nearby olives may feed on it as well. Olives also search for prey such as other mollusks and small crustaceans underneath the sand. Because they locate prey chemically, eyes are absent or greatly reduced.

Harp Shells

Family Harpidae

Above:
Harpa amouretta,
Love harp,
27 mm

Below:
Harpa major,
Major harp,
85 mm

The harp shell family is small, with only twenty-four known species, some of which are very rarely seen. They are characterized by having shells that are heavy, sturdy, glossy and covered with a detailed pattern of rich oranges, browns and maroons. They also have strong radial ribbing that adds both physical and visual strength to the shell.

Harp shells live in sand, silt and mud and are most often encountered just after dark at moderate depths where they come to the surface of the sand to forage for crabs. The harp shell literally pounces on its prey in slow motion so as not to alert the crab, enveloping it with its strong muscular foot and then suffocating it by secreting mucus onto the crab's face and incapacitating its gills.

This group has the ability to self-amputate the posterior part of its foot to escape predation, much like a lizard may drop its tail when threatened. This may distract the predator long enough for the harp shell to burrow to safety under the sand.

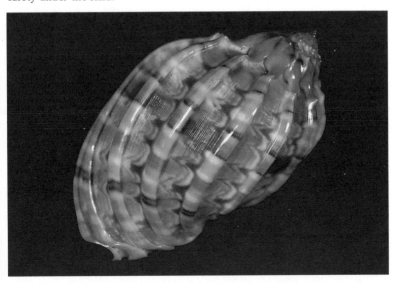

Miters

Family Mitridae

Above:
Mitra fulvescens,
Tawny miter,
35 mm

Below left:
Mitra incompta,
Tessellate miter,
68 mm

Below center:
Mitra mitra,
Episcopal miter,
86 mm

Below right:
Mitra papalis,
Papal miter,
75 mm

The common family name, miter, has come from the perceived resemblance to a Catholic bishop's tall, ornamented headdress. Two distinguishing features of this group are its spindle shape and the folds or teeth on the inner lip (columella). Miter shells are quite variable and range in size from a few millimeters to over 150 mm, with colors ranging from the spectacular orange of the common *Mitra mitra* to the usual browns of most sand-dwelling shells.

Miters are found in a very diverse range of habitats—buried in sand or living among the rocks and corals of the reef. They all possess a long, retractable proboscis which they use to locate food, feeding on everything from worms and clams to detritus. Some will also scavenge the carcasses of dead animals. The larger species are easily found by following their trails in the sand to the end. They are most active at night, but those shells occupied by hermit crabs are most likely seen by day.

Ribbed Miters

Family Costellariidae

These are among the most elegantly colored and shaped of all the miter shells. Long and sleek, they have strong axial ridges and broad spiral bands of color.

Like all miters, they are predatory, living their entire lives buried in sand where they hunt worms and other mollusks. An extremely long and flexible proboscis may be as long as the shell. With it they inject a venom into their prey to paralyze it, then consume it. They can occasionally be seen on the surface of the sand at night when they are hunting more actively.

They are preyed on by rays that fan the sand with their wings, sending the hapless miters tumbling. The ray then sucks them into its mouth where they are crunched up by its hard teeth and powerful jaws. Generally just the animal is eaten by the ray and the broken shell drops back to the bottom where pieces are often found by divers. The empty shells are also found with holes drilled by other mollusks.

Above:
Vexillum suluense,
Sulu miter,
20 mm

Below left:
Vexillum vulpecula,
Little fox miter,
47 mm

Below center:
Vexillum rugosum,
Rugose miter,
38 mm

Below right:
Vexillum plicarium,
Plaited miter,
45 mm

Vase Shells

Family Turbinellidae

The vase shells are a small, but very rugged group of snails which have evolved to withstand the rigors of life in the intertidal zone. There they are exposed during low tides and forced to move into tide pools or fasten tightly to the substrate. At high tides they are pounded mercilessly by the surf as they hunt their prey.

Not surprisingly, the shell is heavily encrusted and the color pattern completely obscured, except on the underside where the shell remains glossy through frequent contact with the animal. There are three to five solid square teeth on the columella (inner lip), presumably to deter would-be predators.

Vase shells are predatory, feeding primarily on worms and rock-dwelling bivalves. These shells are so robust that the empty shells are often found unbroken on beaches and in the shallows at low tide, occupied by hermit crabs. These are desirable fortresses to hermit crabs, often seen vying for the right to occupy a dead vase shell.

Turrids

Family Turridae

While there is no characteristic turrid shape, these shells do share one very curious feature—they all have a notch or slip on the outside of the lip of the shell much like that seen in the strombs, except thinner. It may run deeply into the shell's lip or be barely visible.

Turrids are by far the largest family group and also one of the oldest, being represented in the fossil record as long ago as 135 million years, during the Cretaceous Period. During this long presence on Earth, they have occupied every geographic locality from the poles to the tropics, and an amazing range of habitats from tide pools to the depths of the ocean, living in sand or under rocks.

Though many are very small (2–10 mm), some species, such as one specimen from Japanese waters, can reach 160 mm. They feed on a variety of foods, either by engulfing or stinging their prey. Some even have a venomous harpoon similar to that of the cone shells, with which to spear and immobilize their prey.

Above:
Turris babylonia,
Babylonia turrid,
75 mm

Below left:
Tritonoturris cumingii,
Cuming's turrid,
19 mm

Below center:
Lophiotoma polytropa,
Keeled turrid,
43 mm

Below right:
Turridrupa cerithina,
Cerith-like turrid,
20 mm

Cone Shells

Family Conidae

Above:
Conus vexillum,
Flag cone,
102 mm

Opposite:
Top left:
Conus textile,
Textile cone,
83 mm

Top center:
Conus marmoreus,
Marbled cone,
80 mm

Top right:
Conus geographus,
Geography cone,
99 mm

Bottom left:
Conus magus,
Magus cone,
47 mm

Bottom center:
Conus generalis,
General cone,
53 mm

Bottom right:
Conus aurisiacus,
Aurisiacus cone,
44 mm

The cone shell family has a distinctive, easily recognized shape and contains several very beautiful and colorfully-patterned members. Cone shells are found in all habitats from shallow to moderate depths. The sand-dwelling species possess very clean shells, while those that live out on top of the sand or among rocks or rubble have shells whose patterns are obscured by a layer called the periostracum. Resembling thin brown moss in some species, this layer prevents organisms from growing on the shell and helps to camouflage it. Most are crepuscular (active at twilight or just before dawn) or nocturnal.

They are specialized feeders, preying on worms, mollusks and small fish. All cones have venom glands or are capable of reaching all parts of their shell to defend themselves against carnivorous mollusks. The primary use of the venom is to immobilize their prey which is then swallowed whole. The barbed teeth, which look like arrows, are released when a worm or snail is fired upon, but when the intended prey is a fish, which could swim away, the cone shell holds onto the tooth until the venom takes effect. These teeth can be as long as 10–20 mm in the large fish-eating species such as *Conus striatus* and *Conus geographus*!

While there are many shell-eating fish, cones are the only shells which are known to strike back. The siphon, extending above the surface of the sand, senses a fish above. The proboscis then moves up to the surface of the sand and fires a venom-filled tooth into the fish. The other end of the tooth is held by the shellfish until the fish stops moving. The venom affects the nervous system causing muscular incoordination and eventually respiratory failure. The cone then rears up above the sand and engulfs the fish whole. The same symptoms occur whether the victim is a worm or a human. Some large cones are capable of killing a person within five minutes. Less serious symptoms include paralysis and intense pain.

44

45

Augers

Family Terebridae

Above:
Hastula lanceata,
Lance auger,
40 mm

Below left:
Terebra crenulata,
Crenulate auger,
89 mm

Below center:
Terebra dimidiata,
Dimidiate auger,
100 mm

Below right:
Terebra maculata,
Marlinspike,
78 mm

Auger shells often give away their presence by the furrow created as they plow through sand. While intuitively it would seem that the pointed end leads the way, it is the wider end, where the animal protrudes, which pulls the shell through the sand.

Augers are carnivorous and feed on various types of sand-dwelling worms. Some engulf their prey whole and some have a venom gland to rapidly immobilize the worm. During the day, when auger shells are beneath the sand, a siphon extends to the surface of the sand so that the snail can "breathe" and wastes can be excreted.

Augers can withdraw far enough into their shells that crabs and fish are often unable to reach them. Some crabs and predators such as eagle rays, however, are capable of crushing the shell. Occasionally they succeed only in snapping off the pointed end. Other predatory snails are capable of drilling a hole through the shell to get at the animal inside.

Sundials

Family Architectonicidae

The name of this family comes from the Greek word *architekton*, which means master-builder, in reference to the beautiful construction of these shells.

Since they are sand-dwellers, these finely detailed snails remain clean and glossy. Sundials come out only at night to feed on corals and sea anemones, but can sometimes be found by wading in shallow water among sea grass in the evening and looking for their distinctive round coiling shape. The small nodules of the spiraling underside and the deep umbilicus resemble a miniature circular staircase, and sometimes juvenile sundials can be found inside this umbilicus!

Though not always easy to find, they are one of the most common shells in shell markets where they are sold by the basket-full at very low prices. Like the money cowrie, it would not be surprising to find that populations of sundials have been completely destroyed by commercial harvesting for the trinket trade.

Above and below: *Architectonica perspectiva*, Clear sundial, 36 mm

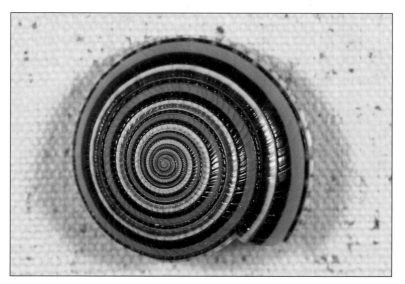

Bubble Shells

Family Cephalaspidae

Above:
Bulla vernicosa,
Varnished bubble,
38 mm

Below left:
Hydatina amplustre,
Royal bubble,
18 mm

Below center:
Atys naucum,
White Pacific bubble,
29 mm

Below right:
Hydatina physis,
Green-lined bubble,
20 mm

Bubble shells have a distinctive wedge-shaped head shield helpful in the burrowing habit of many of these mollusks. Lateral growths of the foot wrap up over the shell, giving the animal a flowing shape as it moves just below the surface of the sand. There are no tentacles and the eyes are sunk into the head shield, both aiding in streamlining.

Bubble shells may possess a lightweight, globose shell which cannot contain the whole animal or an exposed, well-calcified, spiral shell into which the animal can withdraw completely. Other families possess a thinner, smaller shell which the animal envelopes or encloses completely.

Although most are dully-colored sand-dwellers, some are beautiful and live out in the open. Bubble shells can be found in tide pools, especially at night, and to greater depths. Some have well-developed sensory structures allowing them to locate worms and mollusks, and others are herbivores.

Tusk Shells

Family Dentaliidae

Tusk shells, which look like miniature elephant tusks, live buried more or less vertically in sand. Their shells are open at both ends. The tapered end projects just above the sand surface where water is circulated into a long mantle cavity for breathing and waste removal. After several minutes of very slow water inhalation, muscular contraction of the foot expels the water from the same opening. The foot protrudes from the opposite end.

Once the tusk shell has burrowed into the sand, contractions and extensions of the foot pack the sand, creating a small cavity in which the tusk shell can feed. Long tentacles extend from the "head" and explore the cavity for organic debris, protozoans and bivalve larvae which stick to the adhesive ends of the tentacles and are passed back to the mouth. Living tusk shells are rarely seen, but many are washed up on beaches, indicating that they are numerous. Shells in this family were used for currency and ornamentation by North American Indians.

Below left:
Dentalium aprinum,
Boar's tusk,
88 mm

Below right:
Dentalium elephantinum,
Elephant tusk,
76 mm

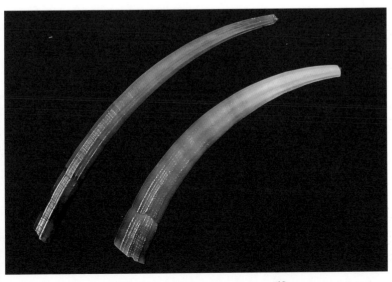

Ark Clams

Family Arcidae

Above:
Barbatia amygdalumtostum,
Almond ark,
35 mm

Bottom left:
Barbatia velata,
Veiled ark,
32 mm

Bottom right:
Arca ventricosa,
Ventricose ark,
44 mm

This family is characterized by a shell the shape of folded bird wings and many tiny teeth along the hinge plate. The hinge is flat or slightly concave and often as long as the shell.

One of the most common species, *Arca ventricosa*, is most noticeable when it snaps its valves shut upon sensing a disturbance. The clam then abruptly pulls itself down into a cavity that it hollowed out in the rock as it was growing, locking itself in place as a protection against predation. To feed, it raises itself up on its muscular foot and opens its two valves enough to filter food from the water.

Although very strongly attached to the rocks while nestled into their custom-built cavities, slipper lobsters are able to pry them loose. This often results in a large pile of empty ark clam shells outside the lobster's current shelter. Eagle rays have also been observed ripping them from the rocks.

Pearl Oysters

Family Pteriidae

The pearl oysters are named for their pearly, opalescent interior lining. This smooth lining is created by very fine layers of aragonite, a form of calcium, which may consist of as many as 5,000 layers of crystals, and is the hardest part of the shell. When the mantle, which lays down this hard layer, becomes irritated by a foreign body such as a grain of sand, it responds by smoothing over the irritant and sometimes completely encasing it in the "pearly" secretion, thus producing a pearl. While pearls can be produced by many mollusks, the most desirable are produced by pearl oysters. The production of the pearl is what gives the inner layer its most common name, "the mother-of-pearl."

Some pearl oysters can be found attached to the reef while others can be seen attached to the limbs of black coral where they are suspended off the bottom. This provides cleaner, steadier flows of water to filter for their food and raises them out of reach of bottom-dwelling predators.

Above:
Pteria penguin,
Penguin wing oyster,
35 mm

Below:
Pinctada margaritifera,
Pearl oyster,
110 mm

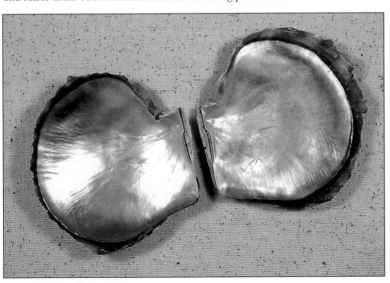

Scallops

Family Pectinidae

Above:
Chlamys cuneatus,
Cuneate scallop,
19 mm

Below top:
Cryptopecten pallium,
Royal cloak scallop,
41 mm

Below bottom left:
Mirapecten mirificus,
Miraculous scallop,
23 mm

Below bottom right:
Decatopecten
noduliferus,
Nodular scallop,
24 mm

These bivalve mollusks have two more or less equal-sized hinged shells, which can be opened and closed. Some scallops spend their lives attached to the bottom, often on the undersides of rocks where they filter water for their food, while other species simply lie out in the open on sand or mud bottoms. When the latter are disturbed, they literally take flight, swimming away from the disturbance in a frantic scramble like a startled flock of birds. A single, huge adductor muscle allows the scallop to rapidly pump its valves together and jet away.

Just inside the scallop's two ruffled shell valves and arrayed along the very edge of the mantle that secretes the shell are hundreds of tiny blue eyes. These are the triggers that start the explosive swimming of the scallop and direct it to swim away from a detected disturbance. This same swimming mechanism produces a jet of water through the siphon allowing it to dig out shallow depressions in the sea bottom in which to lie.

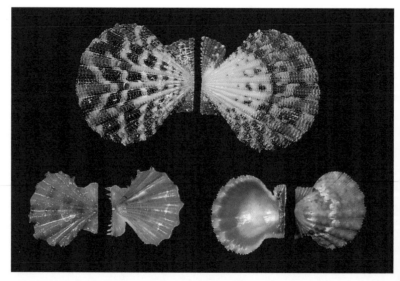

Thorny Oysters

Family Spondylidae

The species in this group are difficult to identify because each shell is so variable. Each oyster, being attached to one spot on the reef for life, encounters different environmental influences such as space limitations, nutrient content of the water and amount of water movement. Therefore, each shell can look quite different from another of the same species and will not necessarily be as symmetrical as most other groups of bivalves.

The many fine or heavy spines along the edge protect the animal from attacks by fish. They also allow places of attachment for algae, tube worms, sponges and other invertebrates which may aid in camouflage, but also add to the difficulty in identification.

This is a vividly-colored group of bivalves, but as with the giant clams, the animal is just as beautiful as the shell in some species. These ruffled, colorful animals, with their many silver, light-sensitive "eyes" along the open edge of the oyster shell, are mesmerizing to watch.

Below left:
Spondylus tenebrosus,
Dark thorny oyster,
67 mm

Below right:
Spondylus sinensis,
Chinese thorny oyster,
62 mm

File Clams

Family Limidae

Above:
Ctenoides ales,
Wandering lima,
61 mm

Below top:
Lima lima,
Spiny lima,
70 mm

Below bottom:
Limaria orientalis,
Oriental lima,
47 mm

Living file clams are most recognized by their thin, delicately-sculpted white shells and the long red or white tentacles which line the mantle edge. Highly sensitive, the extended tentacles can warn of danger and also capture food. When swimming these tentacles expand, adding size to the shell and creating a very pleasing pattern to an onlooking diver. The tentacles are also very sticky and can be dropped by the clam like a lizard drops its tail. A predator attacking the clam is likely to get a mouth full of tentacles for its efforts.

File clams typically live under rocks and down inside dark crevices, but can swim if disturbed. By clapping its valves together, the clam produces a jet of water that allows it to escape. A bottom-dwelling predator such as a starfish has no way of pursuing the jetting clam and, since it lacks eyes, wouldn't even know which direction the clam had taken. File clams are known to build nests created by fibers secreted by their mantle.

Cockles

Family Cardiidae

Though some cockles have heavy, deeply-sculpted shells and others delicate, thin shells, all basically resemble a heart in shape which led to their family name Cardiidae.

Cockles are sand-dwellers which, like many other clams, laterally compress their foot so that it can be pushed deep into the sand, then expand it to work as an anchor as the shell is pulled deep beneath the surface of the sand for protection. Once in a secure place, they extend their siphons back above the sand surface and draw a steady flow of water down to be filtered for food.

Prominent interlocking teeth along the edges of the valves keep most predators out, although the starfish simply grasps the shell from the outside and exerts a continuous pressure, tiring the muscle holding the shells together. Eventually it opens the clam far enough to insert its stomach and digests the living animal in its shell. While the sexes are separate in most bivalves, some cockle species possess both male and female reproductive organs.

Above:
Fragum unedo,
Unedo cockle,
39 mm

Below top:
Trachycardium orbita,
Orbit cockle,
60 mm

Below bottom:
Trachycardium enode,
Enode cockle,
42 mm

True Oysters

Family Ostreidae

Perhaps the most well-known of all bivalves and a major source of seafood worldwide are the oysters. These sedentary mollusks cement their left shell to a hard surface or to the shell of another oyster in areas with good water flow, where they live by filter feeding. So many animals in a small area means good water circulation is critical to carry away wastes. They may also be seen exposed to the air at low tide. During this time, they remain closed, conserving moisture until the tide rises. Because the oyster cannot move from its attachment site, the shell's growth is limited by space and therefore oysters lack the symmetrical shape of many other bivalves.

When mating, they release smoky clouds of gametes into the water in small puffs which then spread out and drift off in the current, stimulating others to do the same. The potential offspring are then carried off in the current. If the colony is large enough, this mating practice can significantly reduce the local underwater visibility.

Tellin Clams

Family Tellinidae

Tellins are a shell collector's nightmare. Many very beautiful and richly-colored species make this one of the most colorful groups of bivalves, but there are also many small white species that are almost impossible to differentiate.

Tellins are quite active, burrowing into the sand with their large foot and extending long siphons up to the surface, one to draw water down to be filtered for food, and the other through which to exhale the water. In addition to filter feeding, some tellins will sometimes extend one very long siphon up onto the surface of the sand at low tide and "vacuum" deposited material, which is sorted in the gills for anything edible. They will often move laterally beneath the sand while searching for new areas to feed after having exhausted the food in an area.

The unusual shape and sculpture of the group may help to keep them from being pulled upward when the siphons are retracted. Because the shells are so thin, concentric growth folds are easily discerned.

Above:
Tellina staurella,
Cross tellin,
36 mm

Below:
Tellina disculus,
Disk tellin,
76 mm

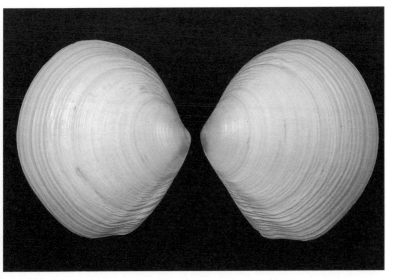

Jewel Boxes

Family Chamidae

Above:
Chama pacifica,
Pacific jewel box,
57 mm

Below:
Chama lazarus,
Lazarus jewel box,
96 mm

The jewel boxes get their name from the upper valve of the shell which forms a lid over the larger lower valve. These shells are not mobile reef- or sediment-dwellers, but cement themselves to rocks or any other hard surface. When growing on old metal shipwrecks they are sometimes shed along with the flaking rust of the hull and fall to the bottom. The shells from these old wrecks often have picked up minerals from the rusting metal and their shells can be orange, yellow, purple or even red. The variable colors combined with the concentric rows of spines make these shells very complex and interesting.

They are all filter feeders and tend to live in colonies. Many factors trigger spawning, including water temperature, tides and chemicals released by other clams. When spawning occurs, the water above these colonies appears to be filled with smoke, as they all release their gametes into the water in synchrony, increasing the chances of fertilization.

Venus Clams

Family Veneridae

The family of Venus clams has been very successful and includes hundreds of species. These clams have thick, hard shells which are generally substantial enough to survive being washed up on beaches and are thus commonly found by beachcombers even in areas of high surf.

They live a sedentary life well-anchored just beneath the surface of sand or mud. From this well-anchored position, they extend a siphon up to the surface of the substrate through which water is drawn for respiration and from which food is filtered. Most of the food consists of microscopic algae which live as plankton. The algae, as well as other assorted items, are trapped by mucus and must be sorted for digestion or disposal.

The bold sculpture of some species indicates that the clams most likely live in sand and may be occasionally subjected to heavy surf where the sculpturing may help to keep them in position while they feed. The almost glassy smooth species are found in more protected areas.

Above:
Lioconcha castrensis,
Camp venus,
46 mm

Below top:
Periglypta magnifica,
Magnificent venus,
54 mm

Below bottom:
Periglypta reticulata,
Reticulate venus,
53 mm

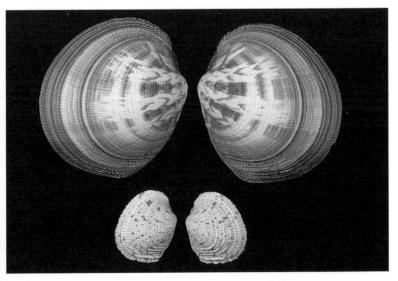

Giant Clams

Family Tridacnidae

Above:
Tridacna squamosa,
Fluted giant clam,
75 mm

Below left:
Tridacna maxima,
Elongate giant clam,
71 mm

Below right:
Tridacna crocea,
Crocus giant clam,
84 mm

Giant clams cannot be truly appreciated unless seen alive. The shells of most, while impressively large, are a plain, chalky white. The true beauty is in the very thick and colorful animal which contains pigments of brilliant green, blue, purple and red.

Giant clams filter food from the water but are also "farmers." Algae living in the clam's tissue supply it with energy. Organs in the clam's mantle focus the sunlight so that several layers of algae can grow simultaneously. Therefore giant clams are found in shallow water with their gapes directed toward the surface and their mantles extended over the edges of the shells for maximum sun exposure. Giant clams are also home to a shrimp which lives in the mantle cavity for protection.

The largest clam known, *Tridacna gigas*, can attain a meter in length and weigh as much as 1100 kg! These clams are now being grown commercially for food to reduce harvesting of wild populations.

Chambered Nautilus

Family Nautilidae

A living relic, the chambered nautilus first appeared in the Cambrian period 600 million years ago when the first abundant marine life existed. Today they inhabit only very deep water—to at least 750 m. At night they travel into shallower water and extend their tentacles to sniff out and feel out their food of crustaceans or other animal remains. Although the nautilus possesses large eyes, it uses mainly smell and touch to locate food.

The name chambered nautilus comes from the distinct chambers within the shell that are filled with gas and serve as flotation for the weight of the shell and animal. Thus, the animal can remain neutrally buoyant at any depth and jet propulsion is used for directional movement and not needed for buoyancy. This ability to swim, unusual for a seashell, allows a greater feeding range and ability to evade predators than if it were sedentary. While not likely to be encountered alive, their shells periodically wash up on beaches.

Above:
Nautilus pompilius,
Chambered nautilus,
90 mm

Below:
Nautilus scrobiculatus,
Umbilicate nautilus,
170 mm

Index

Index

Index